CONTENTS

KW-325-679

Words in **bold** are in the glossary.

Mountain predators

The mountains are a **biome** where land rises above flat earth and foothills. The mountains have forests, lakes and rocky **terrain**. Mountain ranges are the perfect habitat for a predator like the wolf. Wolves have access to prey such as elk and mountain goats.

A grey wolf hunts for prey.

Mountain life

Life in the mountains can be difficult. The air is cold, and there isn't as much oxygen at high **altitudes**. But the mountains are home to some tough predators, including wolves and eagles. Wolves often hunt and roam in the mountains of North America, Europe, Asia and Greenland. Golden eagles soar in mountainous areas of North America, Europe, Asia and North Africa.

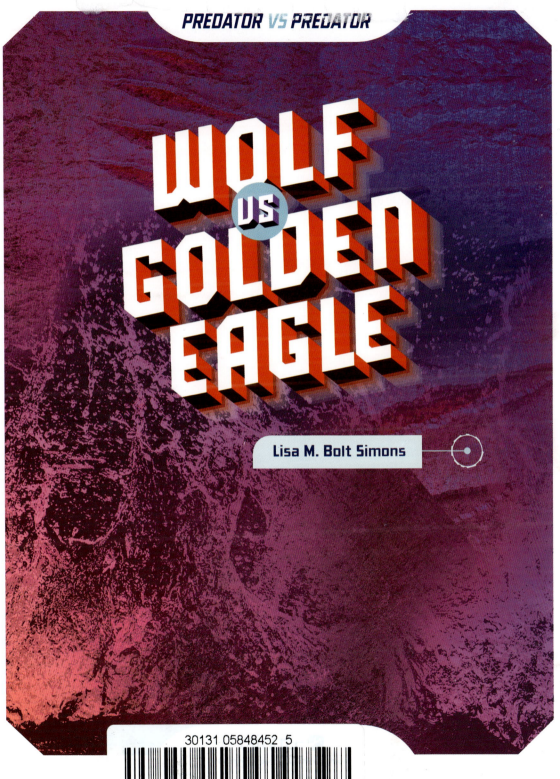

PREDATOR VS PREDATOR

WOLF VS GOLDEN EAGLE

Lisa M. Bolt Simons

Raintree is an imprint of Capstone Global Library Limited, a company incorporated in England and Wales having its registered office at 264 Banbury Road, Oxford, OX2 7DY – Registered company number: 6695582

www.raintree.co.uk
myorders@raintree.co.uk

Edited by Julie Gassman and Aaron Sautter
Designed by Elyse White
Original illustrations © Capstone Global Library Limited 2022
Picture research by Kelly Garvin
Production by Tori Abraham
Originated by Capstone Global Library Ltd
Printed and bound in India

978 1 3982 3544 1 (hardback)
978 1 3982 3543 4 (paperback)

British Library Cataloguing in Publication Data
A full catalogue record for this book is available from the British Library.

Acknowledgements
We would like to thank the following for permission to reproduce photographs:
Dreamstime: Juan Pablo Fuentes Serrano, 17; Getty Images: twildlife, top let 28; Newscom: Patrick Endres, 21; Shutterstock:Alex Jackson, 16,Andrey_Kuzmin, (claw) design element, Andrey_Kuzmin, (metal) design element, Bildagentur Zoonar GmbH, 7, Bonma Suriya, (texture) design element, David Kalosson, 8, Denis Pepin, 13, HaseHoch2, (lightning) design element, HelloRF Zcool, 9, Holly Kuchera, 4, Jearu, 20, Kletr, Cover, middle 6, middle 10, middle 14, middle 18, middle 22, Marc Herrmann, 15, Michal Ninger, 24, top right 28, Michele Aldeghi, 11, Paolo-manzi, 5, Peter Ivanyi, Cover, top 6, top 10, top 14, top 18, top 22, Rayko Tchalkov, 25, ReVelStockArt, (font) design element, Ronnie Howard, 23, Sergei Bachlakov, 27, SergeyBitos, (frame) design element, SerGRAY, design element, Vlada Cech, 12, WinWin artlab, Zhecho Planinski, 19

Every effort has been made to contact copyright holders of material reproduced in this book. Any omissions will be rectified in subsequent printings if notice is given to the publisher.

A golden eagle searches for food.

Like the wolf, the golden eagle also has many choices for prey in the mountains. This **raptor** eats foxes and even white-tailed deer.

Wolves and golden eagles are predators because they eat other animals. The hunted animals are called prey. In order to survive, prey and predators depend on each other in their **ecosystems**. The prey **evolves** over time as it tries to escape or defend itself from the predator. But predators' speed, **endurance**, strength and hunting abilities evolve to help them survive too.

CHAPTER 1

Stellar speed

SPEED

ENDURANCE

STRENGTH

STEALTH

SENSES

WOLF SPEED

GOLDEN EAGLE SPEED

The wolf is not the quickest four-legged hunter on Earth. The golden eagle is not the fastest flyer. But these mountain predators still capture prey with speedy skill.

The wolf is the largest **canid species**. Wolves are larger than jackals, dingoes and domestic dogs. The jackal and greyhound run faster than the wolf. But the wolf's top speed is still 58 to 61 kilometres (36 to 38 miles) per hour. Wolves often hunt white-tailed deer. The deer can run 48 km (30 miles) per hour. It is no match for the wolf.

The elk runs faster than the wolf at 64 km (40 miles) per hour. But a pack of wolves working together can surround an elk and take it as prey.

The canid family

Canids include 35 species of wolves, coyotes, foxes, jackals, dingoes and domesticated dogs. Wolves make up the largest member of the canid family. The most **endangered** species is the red wolf. There are only about 20 that live in North Carolina, USA. Fewer than 250 red wolves live in protected parts of the USA.

The golden eagle can't run like the wolf. But it sometimes hunts prey on the ground. The raptor flaps its wings wildly while it hops and runs to capture prey such as rabbits.

The golden eagle's real speed is found in the sky. But it's not the swiftness of the eagle's flight that makes it deadly. It's how fast the golden eagle dives. This mountain predator streaks towards the ground at more than 241 km (150 miles) per hour!

Golden eagles also hunt pronghorns. These animals run up to 97 km (60 miles) per hour. The golden eagle can easily swoop down on the pronghorn and grab it with its sharp talons.

Golden eagles hunt both small and large animals.

A golden eagle spots its prey and swoops towards it.

Eyries

Golden eagles are the top predator in the north and west of Scotland. They nest on the edges of rocky cliffs or in trees. Their huge nests are called eyries. Cliff nests can be up to 1.5 m (5 feet) across and up to 2 m (6.5 feet) high.

 **Outstanding endurance**

SPEED

ENDURANCE

STRENGTH

STEALTH

SENSES

WOLF ENDURANCE

GOLDEN EAGLE ENDURANCE

The golden eagle isn't just a fast flyer. It also has great endurance. This mountain predator is able to stay in the air for many hours searching for prey. Marmots live in pastures high up in the mountains. When the golden eagle spots them, it dives, grasps a marmot in its talons, and soars off to eat its prey.

Golden eagles often have wingspans more than 2.1 m (7 feet) wide.

Golden eagles also have long-distance endurance. They are able to fly 80 to 201 km (50 to 125 miles) a day. Sometimes they will fly for thousands of kilometres. Some golden eagles migrate south if snow and cold winds last a long time. They also fly south if their prey hibernates, and they need to find food.

Wolves also have great endurance. They need it as they hunt for food. Wolves can trot up to 8 km (5 miles) per hour and may travel 48 km (30 miles) a day or more. These skills are helpful if the wolf is tracking a mountain goat. Wolves hunt in areas as small as 80 square km (50 square miles) or as large as 1,609 square km (1,000 square miles).

Wolves can travel long distances while searching for prey.

FACT

One relative of the wolf is called the Ethiopian wolf. It lives in the mountains of Ethiopia in Africa.

A wolf's large paws help it travel over snow.

The wolf's body is perfectly built for this kind of travel. It has long, powerful legs to take lengthy steps. The wolf's elbows turn inwards, and its large paws help it to balance while travelling over rough ground. Wolves' bodies are thin and muscular, which helps them quickly travel over land and through water.

CHAPTER 3

Strong and mighty

SPEED

ENDURANCE

STRENGTH

STEALTH

SENSES

WOLF STRENGTH

GOLDEN EAGLE STRENGTH

Both the wolf and the golden eagle are strong and mighty. The wolf's strongest body parts are in its mouth.

The wolf has strong jaws. They easily snatch small prey such as beavers and snowshoe hares. But their mighty jaws can also bring down large prey such as elk and moose. The wolf needs its muscular jaws to tear into these big beasts. The predator's jaws are so powerful that they can bite through a moose's leg.

Wolves have sharp teeth and large, powerful jaws.

Wolves also have strong teeth. Their canine teeth, or fangs, can grip prey or tear through fur or skin. The wolves' molars can grind or crush bone.

One of the golden eagle's best weapons is its talons. They are made from the same material as human fingernails. Talons grow up to 7.6 centimetres (3 inches) long and are curved and deadly.

Golden eagles use their razor-sharp talons to catch and kill prey. When the golden eagle's talons strike prey such as squirrels, the force is like a bullet. Golden eagles also use their talons to catch other birds, such as falcons, flying in the air.

Eagle talons are long, sharp and deadly.

A golden eagle eats its prey on a rock.

Golden eagles also have strong, sharp beaks. The hunters use their beaks to rip their prey to pieces so it can be swallowed.

FACT

In the United States, it is a crime to own any part of an eagle without a permit. If someone is caught with an eagle's feather or other body part, they have to pay a fine of up to $200,000, go to prison for one year, or both.

CHAPTER 4

In pursuit

SPEED

ENDURANCE

STRENGTH

STEALTH

SENSES

WOLF STEALTH

GOLDEN EAGLE STEALTH

The golden eagle and the wolf pursue their prey in different ways. The golden eagle mostly stalks prey from the skies. This winged hunter soars high to stalk big prey such as bighorn sheep. It keeps low to hunt prey such as snakes.

The raptor also searches for its next meal from high perches such as trees and rock ledges. Sometimes a pair of golden eagles will hunt together. One golden eagle will chase prey such as a jackrabbit towards its waiting partner.

Two golden eagles share their prey.

Golden eagles sometimes become scavengers when they eat the **carrion** they've found. Golden eagles also steal eggs from nests. Or they may fight other birds to steal their food.

Wolves also stalk their prey. But they usually hunt animals with other wolves in their pack.

Wolves mostly eat **ungulates**, or hoofed mammals. These mammals range from smaller sheep to the huge moose. Because their prey can be so large, the wolves pick animals that are weak. Weak moose include the sick or injured, old or young. The wolf pack tries to separate a weak moose from its herd. The wolves surround the moose and bite its legs, shoulders, sides and nose until it falls.

Wolves mainly hunt animals with hooves, such as deer.

A pack of wolves prepares to attack a moose and its young calf.

Wolves also hunt animals that are slowed down by the habitat. If an elk is stuck in snow, wolves will stalk it and attack.

   # Sensational senses

SPEED

ENDURANCE

STRENGTH

STEALTH

SENSES

WOLF SENSES

GOLDEN EAGLE SENSES

The wolf and the golden eagle have incredible senses. They add to the animals' speed, endurance, strength and stealth.

Wolves develop a sharp sense of smell at only two weeks old. A wolf's sense of smell is about 100 times stronger than a human's. They can smell a herd of caribou from almost 3.2 km (2 miles) away.

Wolves howl to communicate with others over long distances.

The wolf also has an amazing sense of hearing. It can hear birds or other prey in a mountain forest 9.7 km (6 miles) away. If the wolf is in an open meadow, it may hear prey 16 km (10 miles) away.

Howling is a way that this mountain predator communicates. Wolves understand that if they hear the howls of a different pack, it means to stay away.

An eagle's sharp eyesight can spot prey from far away.

The golden eagle has an amazing sense of sight. Golden eagles can use their eyes in different ways. They are able to focus both eyes on the same object the way humans do. This is called **binocular vision**. But eagles also have **monocular vision**. One eye can look straight ahead while the other looks to the side.

FACT

Golden eagles are sometimes used by falconry hunters in central Asia. The birds are trained to catch foxes, deer and antelope.

The golden eagle's long-distance eyesight is astounding. It can see a rabbit running more than 3.2 km (2 miles) away. Golden eagles can also rotate their heads 270 degrees to scan for prey. This ability helps the golden eagle to easily spot a squirrel and head for the kill.

A golden eagle can rotate its head to see what's behind it.

LEGENDARY PREDATORS

The wolf and golden eagle are legendary hunters. They often appear in tales and myths around the world. Stories from Italy, Scandinavia and Turkey feature wolves that are brave and strong. Japanese stories describe noble wolves that protect travellers. Wolves in Native American tales are courageous and successful hunters.

The eagle is also a popular character in different cultures. The bird appears in ancient Greek stories called Aesop's Fables. The golden eagle also plays an important role in Native American ceremonies. US laws allow Native people to use eagle feathers or body parts in headdresses, dance shawls and other items. Some Native people once believed that eagle feathers had the power to give people strength and courage.

Some Native people wear animal skins or
eagle feathers as part of their ceremonies.

WOLF VS **GOLDEN EAGLE**

The golden eagle is a fast hunter when it dives. But the wolf has endurance to travel long distances while hunting. The golden eagle stalks its prey from different heights. The wolf works with its pack to take down prey. The golden eagle has lethal talons. But the wolf's teeth and jaws are strong enough to bite through bone.

Both of these mountain predators are magnificent. Which one would be named the top predator? Is it the wolf? Or is it the golden eagle?

WOLF STATS

HEIGHT: 66 to 81 centimetres (26 to 32 inches)

LENGTH: 1 to 2 metres (4.5 to 6.5 feet)

WEIGHT: up to 59 kg (130 pounds)

BIGGEST EVER RECORDED: 79 kg (175 pounds)

TYPES/SPECIES AROUND THE WORLD:
two main species, grey and red

NUMBER OF TEETH: 42; fangs can be 6 cm (2.5 inches) long

PREY: deer, moose, elk, caribou, bison, sheep, oxen, mountain goats, beavers, hares, fish, mice, squirrels

GOLDEN EAGLE STATS

HEIGHT: 84 to 97 cm (33 to 38 inches)

WINGSPAN: 1.8 to 2.3 m (6 to 7.5 feet)

WEIGHT: up to 7 kg (15 pounds)

BIGGEST EVER RECORDED: 7.7 kg (17 pounds)

TYPES/SPECIES AROUND THE WORLD: 60

NUMBER OF TALONS: 8 in total; can grow to 8 cm (3 inches) long

PREY: squirrels, foxes, birds, snakes, marmots, rabbits, pronghorn, white-tailed deer, fish, coyotes

GLOSSARY

altitude how high a place is above sea level

binocular vision ability to use both eyes to focus on something

biome community of plants and animals in a major region of the planet

canid animal in the dog family, including wolves, hyenas, coyotes, foxes and domesticated (pet) dogs

carrion dead and decaying animals

ecosystem group of animals and plants that work together with their surroundings

endangered at risk of dying out

endurance ability to keep doing an activity for long periods of time

evolve change gradually over long periods of time

monocular vision ability to look at or focus on something using only one eye

raptor bird of prey that hunts and eats other animals

species group of animals or plants that share common characteristics

terrain surface and features of the land

ungulate four-footed mammal that has hooves and usually eats plants

FIND OUT MORE

BOOKS

Animals (DKfindout!), DK (DK Children, 2016)

Birds (DKfindout!), DK (DK Children, 2019)

Eagles: Built for the Hunt (Predator Profiles), Tammy Gagne (Raintree, 2016)

Wolf: Killer King of the Forest (Top of the Food Chain), Angela Royston (Raintree, 2019)

WEBSITES

www.bbc.co.uk/bitesize/topics/zx882hv/articles/z3c2xnb
What is a food chain? Learn more!

www.dkfindout.com/uk/animals-and-nature
Find out more about animals and nature.

INDEX